RAILW....
ACCIDENTS

Greg Morse

Happy Birthday Rhys,
with all our love,

Bill - Sarah x

Published in Great Britain in 2015 by Shire Publications Ltd, PO Box 883, Oxford, OX1 9PL, UK.

PO Box 3985, New York, NY 10185-3985, USA.

E-mail: shire@shirebooks.co.uk www.shirebooks.co.uk

A CIP catalogue record for this book is available from the British Library.

Shire Library no. 794. ISBN-13: 978 0 74781 371 2
PDF e-book ISBN: 978 1 78442 031 4
ePub ISBN: 978 1 78442 030 7

Greg Morse has asserted his right under the Copyright, Designs and Patents Act, 1988, to be identified as the author of this book.

Designed by Tony Truscott Designs, Sussex, UK and typeset in Garamond Pro and Gill Sans.

Printed in China through Worldprint Ltd.

15 16 17 18   10 9 8 7 6 5 4 3 2

COVER IMAGE

Cover design by Peter Ashley. Front cover: In 1905, two North Eastern Railway (NER) locomotives derailed on the Grand Bank near Gainford, County Durham, after track workers had removed a length of rail. This photograph of the incident was part of a record compiled by the locomotive engineer Edward Thompson when he worked for the NER. (Courtesy of the Science and Society Picture Library). Back cover: Red warning flag, photograph by Peter Ashley.

TITLE PAGE IMAGE

The post-accident scene at Milton, near Didcot. At 1:13 p.m. on 22 November 1955, an excursion from Treherbert to Paddington derailed when the driver failed to slow for a crossover being used to divert services away from engineering works. Eleven people were killed.

CONTENTS PAGE IMAGE

Recovery operations are well under way at Stratton (near Swindon) in November 1958. A freight had come off at the trap points – a 'turnout' used to protect loops and sidings from unauthorised train movements – and its wagons had ended up foul of the main line. They were struck by two other trains, one of which can be seen in the background.

ACKNOWLEDGEMENTS

I am indebted to Julia Jenkins, Roger Badger, the Dacorum Heritage Trust Ltd, Matt Clements, Colour-Rail, D. J. Fleming, Bridget Eickhoff, Graham Floyd, John Foster, Irene Grabowska, Chris Hall, John Heald, Derek Hotchkiss, Philip Hunt, the Kidderminster Railway Museum Trust, Garry Keenor, Mirrorpix, Gerald Riley, STEAM Museum, Debbie Stevens, Slough Library, and Michael Woods. Finally, my thanks are also due to Nick Wright and Russell Butcher at Shire Publications.

Illustrations are acknowledged as follows (by page number):

Roger Badger: 29, 49 (top); Colour-Rail (John E. Henderson): 4; The Dacorum Heritage Trust Ltd: 52 (top); Roy F. Burrows, Midland Collection Trust/ Kidderminster Railway Museum: 12 (bottom), 27; Kidderminster Railway Museum: 15; Mary Evans Picture Library: 10 (top), 11 (bottom), 18, 24, 26 (top), 28, 34; Mirrorpix: 4, 6, 7, 30, 46, 48, 50, 53, 54, 56, 58, 59, 60, 61, 62, 64, 66, 67 (bottom), 69; Greg Morse: 20 (top), 22, 36 (top), 38, 44, 45, 55; The Railways Archive: 40, 70; Science & Society Picture Library: 9, 10 (bottom), 12 (top), 17, 20 (bottom), 23, 32–3; Slough Library: 36 (bottom); STEAM Museum: 1, 3, 11 (top), 16 (top), 26 (bottom), 37, 43, 49 (bottom), 52 (bottom), 65, 67 (top); Westinghouse Archive/Kidderminster Railway Museum: 16 (bottom), 21, 41; Wiki Commons: 13.

Shire Publications is supporting the Woodland Trust, the UK's leading woodland conservation charity, by funding the dedication of trees.

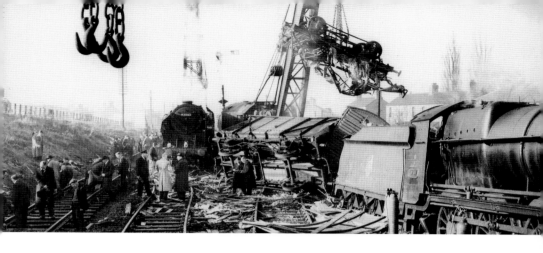

CONTENTS

INTRODUCTION

The red beam burns against the night; the driver stops the train and waits.

WAITING. That's the lot of the goods driver: waiting in a loop for an express to pass by; waiting in a yard for the 'off'. But wait he must – the signal is red and red means danger. It also means safe: red signals warn drivers of points set against them, obstructions up ahead, and of course other trains. So if a driver passes a signal at 'danger' – if there's a *SPAD* – an accident can occur.

But what if a red signal actually shows green? It *should* be impossible; it *is* very rare. Yet that's exactly what happened on 12 December 1988, when a 'phantom aspect'

The railway's sentinel of safety has long been the signal. This 'cantilever' has 'heads' protecting two lines. It looks as though 33211 has committed a 'signal passed at danger' incident – a SPAD. In fact, the signal has returned to red in order to protect the locomotive as it continues its journey.

led a packed rush-hour service into the rear of another near Clapham Junction. The impact forced a passing empty unit off the rails, killed thirty-five people and injured almost five hundred more.

The resulting inquiry found that a live wire had been left dangling in a relay room; when jolted a couple of weeks later, it touched a terminal, made a connection and prevented a signal from returning to 'danger' after the passage of an earlier train. Beneath this surface failure, investigators also found problems with management, supervision, training and rostering. It's a basic truth about accidents: that there's always more than one cause. Thus, at Bellgrove Junction on 6 March 1989, a driver passed a signal at 'danger', true, but the fatal collision that followed would not have come had the guard not given the 'right away' while the red light was still shining, or if BR had not altered the track layout in such a way that a SPAD could put one train into the path of another.

The Clapham collision of 12 December 1988. Here, firemen and engineers are cutting through the wreckage in the search for survivors.

SC75837

In the causal chain of the fatal accident at Bellgrove was the simplification of the junction from a double-track arrangement to one which included a short stretch of single track.

The SPAD at Purley two days before seemed to be an exception to the rule, seemed in fact to be all the driver's fault. After all, it was *he* who took his train past a 'red', *his* mistake that caused it to collide with the rear of another, *his* negligence that killed five people and injured eighty-eight more. That's certainly what the press thought, who pilloried him in their pages, and what the courts thought, who sentenced him to eighteen months in prison. Indeed, the driver himself had never said otherwise, had never done anything but bravely admit his guilt. Except that the truth was not nearly so simple.

The same signal had been passed at 'danger' four times before; such things are seldom coincidental, and often suggest that the position of the gantry or post makes the head prone to being overlooked. In this case, though

The prison sentence of the driver involved in the collision at Purley was reduced from eighteen months to four on appeal, but when the new evidence was presented in 2007, his conviction was overturned. He drowned in a boating accident two years later.

drivers had slightly longer to see the signal while in motion than the seven seconds considered acceptable for a 90-mph line, it became obscured by the station buildings as the train approached. The investigating officer recommended that erecting a repeater would lengthen this 'sighting time' and help cut the number of SPADs at the signal itself. The "new evidence" was accepted by the court in 2007 and the conviction overturned. Sadly, the driver would live with his good name restored for just two more years.

Behind every statistic is a face. These floral tributes were placed at the Clapham crash site by mourners in 1988.

Clapham, Purley and Bellgrove mark 1988–9 as a pivotal period for railway safety. Much technology had been applied to accident prevention by this time; much more would follow. This book charts these developments, along with the checks and balances between investigators and operators, and the abiding need to respect the lessons of the past, both today … and tomorrow.

EARLY DAYS

Those who heard it would remember the sound for the rest of their lives: the crunch of bone, the cry of pain. And it was meant to be such an auspicious day, a great day for Britain ...

NOT THAT THE opening of the Liverpool & Manchester Railway could ever be as joyous as the opening of the Stockton & Darlington in 1825: George IV was now dead, unemployment was rife, and there were concerns about another revolution in France. Yet the Act had been passed, the money had been spent, and the famous Rainhill Trials had demonstrated the value of steam. By 15 September 1830, the stage was well and truly set for the launch of this, the first timetabled passenger line in the world.

Planned as a grand procession, the opening ceremony would feature eight trains, each conveying the great and good from one city to the other at speeds unheard of hitherto. A run in August had shown that the line and its locomotives were ready. Now, at Crown Street station, the crowd was ready, the flags were ready, and the Stephensons were ready too. The new king failed to appear, but the Duke of Wellington, the redoubtable (though none too popular) Prime Minister, did – along with Sir Robert Peel and Liverpool MP William Huskisson, one of the scheme's biggest supporters. They, and some eighty lords, ladies and ambassadors, soon boarded the leading special.

At precisely twenty-to eleven, a cannon boomed and *Northumbrian* hauled the train out towards Manchester, followed – on the adjacent line – by the rest. Waving well-wishers lined the route, and soon the procession was making good progress as it headed through Olive Mount cutting.

By noon, the Duke's train had pulled up at Parkside. Despite warnings from railway staff, around fifty passengers alighted to take in the scene, stretch their legs and chew the fat. Huskisson – politically estranged from Wellington – caught the Prime Minister's eye as he walked past the state carriage. The Duke opened the door and held out his hand, but as Huskisson grasped it, a cry went up – *Rocket* was approaching at alarming speed.

The locomotive had no brake, but the driver threw it hard into reverse. Most clambered back into the train or leapt to the embankment. Huskisson, less agile than many, tried to climb into the carriage, but as he grabbed the door,

The Moorish Arch at Edge Hill, Liverpool, during the opening of the Liverpool & Manchester Railway on 15 September 1830. Note the luxurious state coach, in which the Duke of Wellington was to travel, and which would soon be involved in the world's first rail passenger fatality.

it swung open, throwing him onto the track and into the path of danger. His leg was crushed with a sickening crunch. 'I have met my death,' he murmured as he was carried away. 'God forgive me!'

With great presence of mind, George Stephenson ordered the leading coach to be uncoupled. With Huskisson safely inside, he climbed back on *Northumbrian*'s footplate and opened the regulator wide. The engine managed the 15 miles to Eccles in just twenty-five minutes – an astonishing average speed of 36 mph. From the vicarage there, the surgeons

William Huskisson MP, who was run over and killed by *Rocket*.

An anonymous portrait of George (left) and a youthful Robert (right) Stephenson.

The devastating effect of a boiler explosion may be seen in this shot of the GWR broad-gauge locomotive *Leopard*. Cast-iron wheel breakages also occurred frequently in the early days.

were summoned, but all efforts were in vain: Huskisson died from his wounds later that evening.

Despite this incident – and the press coverage it gained – Victorian enthusiasm remained undimmed: within a few weeks of opening, the Liverpool & Manchester was carrying its first mails; within a year, it would be taking tens of thousands to the Newton races. Such success gave a boon to businessmen elsewhere in Britain, and soon a Parliament keen to stimulate economic growth and speed the transfer of troops was passing Acts to authorise the Sheffield & Manchester (1831), London & Birmingham (1833) and Great Western (1835) railways, among many others.

Operating practices left much to be desired in these pioneering days, and often led to derailments or collisions. The latter were exacerbated by the lack of steam-powered brakes (trains being stopped by manual apparatus on each

The locomotive engineer Timothy Hackworth – rival to the Stephensons at the Rainhill Trials, and inventor of an improved steam safety valve that helped reduce boiler explosions.

Lime Street station, Liverpool, was opened in 1836. Initially, trains were uncoupled from their locomotive at Edge Hill and allowed to coast down the steep incline to Lime Street, controlled by a brakesman. Outgoing trains were connected by rope to a stationary engine, which pulled them back to Edge Hill and a waiting locomotive.

vehicle) and the fact that services were kept apart not by fixed signals, but by 'time interval' working, which involved positioning a railway 'policeman' at a particular point (or 'block post'), so that he could regulate the flow of traffic with hand signals. No problem if watches were accurate and trains kept to timetable, but if either condition were broken, accidents could occur. When services were sparse, trains were light and speeds were low, cases were many but casualties were minimal. The trouble came when the popularity of rail travel created a need for faster, heavier and more frequent services …

An engraving showing a railway policeman undertaking signalling duties at the northern portal of Milford Tunnel in Derbyshire.

AN INSPECTOR CALLS

S EVEN A.M. ON 7 August 1840, and a passenger service leaves Leeds for Hull. At Selby, some twenty miles east, a rake of coaches and a wagon of iron castings are added to the train. The latter is coupled next to the engine, but though its load is precarious, the journey goes well till Howden looms near. Here, the largest casting falls to the track, causing a derailment that kills four passengers.

The accident was a clear case of neglect: those who had positioned the castings had placed the largest piece loosely on some smaller ones and lashed the whole with rope, which was worn away as the train passed over points and joints. There were no chains, no wooden frames; furthermore, the load had not been checked before the journey began.

So much is known about this incident as it was the subject of the first investigation by the Railway Inspectorate (RI).

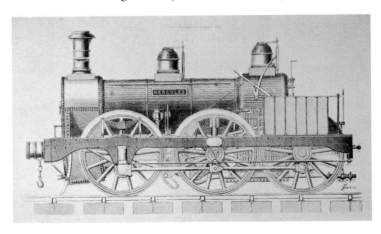

Hercules, a six-wheeled locomotive of the Hull & Selby Railway, on whose metals the first accident to be investigated by the RI occurred. Like all his successors up to the 1980s, the first Inspector-General – Lieutenant-Colonel Sir J. M. Frederic Smith FRS – was a former Royal Engineer.

The Inspector-General, Lieutenant-Colonel Sir J. M. Frederic Smith FRS, considered all the evidence and concluded that it should be the duty of the goods foreman to make sure all merchandise was properly packed and firmly fixed before being placed in a passenger train, adding that it would be desirable if he confirmed in writing immediately before departure that he had done so.

Until Howden, all fatal accidents had been inquired into by a coroner's jury, which could bring a verdict of manslaughter against those it held responsible. The trouble was that these good men and true invariably lacked the expertise to pass judgement on technical matters, which is why Smith and his colleagues were recruited from the Corps of Royal Engineers (most civil engineers already being in the railways' employ). It had also been realised that, as the railways had been granted powers by government to build their lines, government should oversee their rapidly expanding operations – especially where safety was concerned. As a result, it passed the first Railway Regulation Act (1840), which created the RI and required (*inter alia*) all injurious accidents to be reported to the Board of Trade.

The RI would 'provide for the due Supervision of Railways, for the Safety of the Public' and, though its inspectors could 'enter upon and examine' railway works, buildings and rolling stock, they had no actual authority to investigate accidents. This, it was felt, kept the responsibility for managing railways with the railways themselves. Nevertheless, the RI did conduct inquiries and submit reports to Parliament in the hope that companies might be 'persuaded' to adopt safer working methods, better equipment and so on. And 'persuasion' was indeed the right word, the railways' emphasis on making money being matched only by a resentment of interference from 'outsiders'.

This is not to say that no safety improvements came about before the RI came into being: the steam whistle was

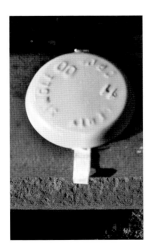

developed in this period, reputedly after a collision between a train and a farmer's cart at Bagworth in May 1833, while in 1841 British engineer Edward Cowper invented the detonator, a small explosive device that, when attached to the track, could be set off by a passing locomotive to warn of imminent danger. Yet signalling remained rudimentary, many signals being ambiguous – some giving no positive 'danger' indication, others no positive 'all clear'. Those designed by Brunel for the Great Western Railway (GWR) were the first to do both and were very successful. Ironic then that the first major accident the RI investigated would be on that line …

A railway detonator (or 'fog signal') – a simple, effective means of warning trains, and much more efficient than putting hot coals on the line or waving one's arms (as had been the practice hitherto).

Imagine yourself a stonemason, working on the new Palace of Westminster. You've toiled for months on this great Victorian masterpiece, but tomorrow is Christmas Day and you're heading home. Perhaps you've enjoyed a draught or two, perhaps you had to run for it. Either way, as you head down the slope into Paddington, you know you'll be on West Country soil again soon. Shame you never make it.

When 4:30 came that morning, the regular Bristol-bound goods left London in darkness. The locomotive – a 2-4-0 named *Hecla* – was hauling two third-class carriages,

A Great Western 'disc and crossbar' signal showing 'all clear'.

The first semaphore signal (London & Croydon Railway, 1841) had three positions, each with a corresponding coloured light: horizontal (red) for 'stop' or 'danger'; diagonally downwards at 45 degrees (green) for 'caution'; and vertical – hidden in a slot in the post – (white) for 'clear'. Note how this later 'three-position', upper quadrant example dispenses with the slot arrangement.

a parcels van and seventeen wagons. Though the train was ten minutes late leaving Twyford, the early part of the journey was uneventful. In fact it wasn't until about seven – when *Hecla* entered the dark cavern of Sonning Cutting, just east of Reading – that some lives changed and other lives ended.

Heavy rain had soaked the ground to such an extent that a great mass of soil had slid down the steep cutting walls to block the line. The driver didn't stand a chance: the engine struck the debris with great force, causing it to derail; the momentum of the heavy goods wagons crushed the third-class carriages up against the tender. Eight people were killed and seventeen were injured (one of whom later died in hospital).

Though Sonning was perhaps the first railway accident to result from natural forces, the GWR's own actions had worsened the consequences. First, its third-class carriages were flimsy, open to the elements and not fitted with sprung buffers, meaning that there was nothing to soften the impact or prevent passengers from being thrown from the train; second, coupling the carriages between heavy goods wagons and a heavy engine worsened the 'telescoping' when the train suddenly stopped.

The GWR later introduced improved third-class vehicles (with sprung buffers) and never positioned them next to the engine in goods trains again. The RI – believing that the weight differentials meant marshalling vehicles designed to carry people with those designed to carry freight was asking for trouble anyway – continued to warn against running carriages in goods trains at all.

Widely reported in the papers, Sonning brought home the dangers of rail travel to the British public. Soon, however, an accident in France would have much further-reaching effects for both public and practitioner alike.

Sonning Cutting, c.1846. The accident here on 24 December 1841 speeded reform for third-class passengers, the Railway Regulation Act of 1844 compelling companies to provide at least one third-class return service a day that used adequate carriages, stopped at all stations, ran at no less than 12 mph, and whose fare cost no more than a penny a mile. Such 'Parliamentary trains' soon proved extremely popular.

FROM TIME TO SPACE

Iᴛ ᴡᴀꜱ ᴛʜᴇ ᴀꜰᴛᴇʀɴᴏᴏɴ of Sunday 8 May 1842, a fete honouring King Louis Philippe was coming to an end, and people were heading home to Paris. At 5:30 p.m., 770 of them left on a train that stretched some 400 feet behind two locomotives. All seemed well, but as the engines worked harder, an axle was growing weaker … By Bellevue it was at breaking point; before Meudon it had snapped, sending the leading engine off the rails and scattering hot coals and ash in all directions. The wooden carriages quickly caught fire. Countless people died; most had burned to death in their locked compartments.

Metal fatigue caused the axle failure, but it was those locked doors that led to public outcry – and the abandonment of the practice in France (even though the fire had spread too quickly for it to have made any real difference to the death toll). Many British companies followed suit; the Great Western, however, felt that locked doors protected the privacy and property of passengers, and also stopped them climbing up to the roof or jumping down to retrieve a hat, as many had done in the slower world of the stagecoach. And maybe they had a point – at least from their own perspective: Great Western trains would soon be covering the 194 miles between Paddington and Exeter in just 4½ hours, averaging an astonishing 46¾ mph. Yet as speeds were increasing, the system was expanding – rapidly.

In 1841, there were 1,556 route miles open to traffic; by 1850 there were 6,621. Passenger numbers also grew from

Opposite:
An oil painting showing
the terrible derailment and fire at Meudon, near Versailles, on 8 May 1842.

Bulkeley, a locomotive of the 'Rover' class, a development of the earlier 'Iron Duke' series. Both types were capable of 80 mph and helped secure the Great Western's early reputation for high speed.

20 to 67 million in the same period, but while fatalities remained miraculously low (nine were killed in 1848, five in 1849, and twelve in 1850), the combination of faster trains, more miles and more journeys brought a corresponding rise in accidents. Some were boiler explosions; some, indeed, resulted from broken axles. Others occurred when wagons rolled from sidings on to running lines. The biggest problem, however, stemmed from 'time interval' working, as a fatal collision on 1 August 1850 would demonstrate all too well.

That day, the Scottish Central Railway was running three excursion trains – five minutes apart – to the Highland Agricultural Society show in Glasgow. When the second one got to Cowlairs, it found the first one waiting – the train was so long it had blocked the points where a shunt was to be made. While the crews discussed what to do, the third train struck the rear of the second, killing five people and injuring ten more.

The RI blamed the accident on the crew's failure to protect

Early telegraph machines used needles to point to a letter of the alphabet on a grid. The fewer the needles – this 1844 example has two – the more each letter was codified and therefore harder to interpret. However, fewer needles also meant simpler wiring and lower installation costs.

The grouping of signal and point levers on to a single frame was introduced at Bricklayers Arms Junction on the London & Croydon Railway in 1843. The interlocking of points and signals followed nine years later, on the Manchester Sheffield & Lincolnshire Railway. Interlocking and frame would first come together on the North London Railway in 1860.

the rear of the second train, which could have been achieved with a hand signal or detonator, though by now there was another option available to the industry: electric telegraph communication. Developed by Charles Wheatstone and Sir William Fothergill Cooke in 1837, an improved version had entered commercial use on the GWR between Paddington and West Drayton on 9 April 1839. Its application to signalling soon followed: in 1842, Cooke suggested splitting lines into sections, each governed

The north portal of Clayton Tunnel, *c.* 1905. The cottage between the turrets was added in 1849, eight years after the tunnel opened, and was originally inhabited by the tunnel keeper, whose duties included keeping the gas lamps in the tunnel lit. Passing trains tended to snuff them out, but as speeds increased, the job became impractical and the lamps were eventually extinguished for good.

by a separate telegraph; a train would not be allowed into a section until the preceding one could be proved to have left it. This 'absolute block system', in which time gave way to the safer parameter of space, was first used on the Norwich to Great Yarmouth line in 1844.

Though favoured by the RI, 'absolute block' was expensive and many companies recoiled at the cost of installation. The same was true of the interlocking of points and signals to prevent conflicting routes being set, the need for which was confirmed by a fatal buffer-stop collision at Burnley in 1852. Some also thought 'lock and block' would dull the alertness of signalmen and train crews, an argument that was lent some weight by an accident on the London Brighton & South Coast Railway (LB&SCR) one Sunday morning in 1861.

Breakfast time on 25 August found Signalman Killick working at Clayton Tunnel South. Clayton was the first tunnel to be protected by telegraph, two machines allowing the boxes at each portal to communicate with each other. The boxes also controlled Distant signals that could be returned to 'danger' either by the signalman

turning a wheel or by a train working
a treadle. If a signal failed, an
alarm bell would sound and the
signalman would resort to using
coloured flags.

Shortly after 8:30 a.m. a
train entered the tunnel, but
the signal stuck in the 'clear'
position and the alarm went
off. Killick tapped out the
'train in tunnel' code to
his colleague Mr Brown at
Clayton Tunnel North, but
by the time he turned his
attention to the bell a second
train was approaching at
speed. Killick managed to
get his red flag out just as the engine disappeared from
view. Once more, he sent 'train in tunnel' to Brown, but
as he did so the first train burst into the sunshine and
thundered past the latter's cabin. Perhaps Brown never
got this second signal; perhaps he got confused. Either
way, he signalled back to Killick that the tunnel was
'clear'. Dripping with relief, Killick showed his white flag
to the third train, whose driver promptly opened up and
powered into the darkness.

The trouble was not so much that the second driver
hadn't seen the 'red', than that he had. Thinking something
was wrong up ahead, he stopped the train and put the
locomotive into reverse. The guard's van was around
250 yards from the tunnel mouth when the third train
struck it. Twenty-three people were killed and 176 were
injured. It was Britain's worst railway accident to date.
It was also a blow to the RI, whose inspectors were urging
the railways to adopt 'absolute block'.

It would be some time before they succeeded.

By 1860, the laborious method of sending telegraph messages letter by letter had been replaced by a two-position instrument designed to show 'Train on Line' or 'Line Clear'. In 1852, C. V. Walker had combined the telegraph with a bell, with which signalmen could describe, 'offer' and 'accept' trains using a set of codes (though these were not standardised until 1884). This instrument dates from c. 1880.

BRIDGES AND BRAKES

CAPTAIN TYLER'S Clayton Tunnel report criticised the signal for its design, the staff at Brighton for dispatching trains too close together, and the absence of a book in which signalmen could record passing times. Much of his censure, however, was reserved for the telegraph machines, which gave no positive indication to show whether the line ahead was occupied, making the signalman's memory the second line of defence – a potentially dangerous arrangement. Worst of all, perhaps, was the fact that unsuitable equipment like this 'prejudiced railway managers against it, in a way materially to hinder its adoption and retard its progress'.

And prejudiced some of them certainly were. The London & North Western Railway (LNWR), for example, was particularly slow to adopt modern safeguards: failure to interlock the signalling with points, as recommended after a fatal collision at Walton Junction in 1862, led to the deaths of eight passengers when a conflicting move let an express strike a stationary coal train at the same location in 1867; failure to link Llandulas and Abergele by telegraph meant that the company's celebrated 'Irish Mail' could not be stopped when a rake of wagons ran away on a steep incline the following year. This time, though, the losses were much greater, thirty-one passengers and two crew losing their lives in the resulting collision and fire.

The 'Irish Mail' was also involved in an accident at Tamworth on 14 September 1870. The signalman expected a goods train, and had set the points for the platform loop.

Opposite:
During shunting operations at Llandulas on 20 August 1868, a rake of wagons (two of which were carrying paraffin) was left on the main line with the brakes not pinned down. When more were fly-shunted on to them, they began to roll back down the incline. As there was no way of sending a message to stop the 'Irish Mail', it struck the wagons head on. Fire engulfed the leading carriages, killing thirty-three people.

On 9 June 1865, a London-bound train derailed near Staplehurst, killing ten people. Maintenance work was under way on Beult Viaduct, but the foreman misread his timetable and thought he had more time. As a result, two lengths of rail had not been replaced before the train reached the site. Among the surviving passengers was Charles Dickens, who was deeply affected by the accident.

SCENE OF THE FATAL ACCIDENT AT STAPLEHURST, ON THE SOUTH-EASTERN RAILWAY.—FROM A SKETCH TAKEN NEXT DAY.

The driver expected a clear run, and kept the speed steady. It wasn't until he saw the signals set for the platform that he realised he was wrong. As he applied the brake, the 'Mail' lurched over from the main line, ran through the loop, crashed through the stop block of the siding beyond and plunged into the River Anker. The driver, his fireman and one passenger were killed. Had a separate 'Distant' arm been

On 5 November 1868, the 5 p.m. mail train from Milford ran into the rear of a cattle train at Newnham, killing four people and injuring six. The line used 'time interval' signalling, but low adhesion caused the cattle train to stall, allowing the 'mail' to catch up.

provided for the loop, the driver would have known which route was set sooner; had 'absolute block' been in use, the signalman would have known which service was next; had the train been equipped with better brakes, it might not have overrun the siding anyway ...

Although there had been experiments with various braking systems since the 1850s, it was not until 1875 that a Royal Commission on the safe working of railways ran a series of trials to ascertain the most suitable design. Eight different companies took part, but the results were largely inconclusive, most systems failing to meet the Board of Trade's requirements that a brake should be capable of fitment to all vehicles in a train, be capable of operation by the guard as well as the driver, and come on automatically if the train divided. While the debate raged on, however, accidents continued to occur – as on the evening of 21 January 1876.

It was one of the worst blizzards in living memory: a harsh gale was blasting huge flakes through fens and farms, as a coal train fought its way from Peterborough. The crew could barely see the signals through the snow, but still they carried on. Ahead was a pall of white; behind was the Up 'Scotch Express'. Like them, it was late; unlike them, it was gaining ground fast.

The signalman at Holme had been told to shunt the 'coal' to let the express pass by, but found to his alarm that the driver ignored the Stop signals and continued

The Abbots Ripton accident of 1876 was partly due to the GNR's use of slotted post signals, whose arms had stuck in the slots, making them appear to read 'clear'. The company later adopted a 'somersault' design, which did away with the slot arrangement altogether.

towards Conington. Thankfully, the Great Northern Railway (GNR) had embraced the telegraph, so he was able to send a message to Abbots Ripton, asking that the shunt be made there instead. Having acknowledged the message, the signalman at Abbots Ripton returned his signals to 'danger', only to see the coal train passing them too. There was nothing for it but to display a red hand-lamp to bring it to a stand. Thankfully, it worked and the train was soon reversing into a siding. A few seconds sooner and they'd have been safe, but six wagons were still on the running line when the express suddenly appeared. After the collision, staff tried to protect the wreckage, but it was too late to stop a Leeds service from striking it and taking the death toll to fourteen.

The investigation revealed that continuous brakes might have stopped the 'Leeds' short of the obstruction, and suggested that the accident might have been avoided altogether if extra precautions – such as reducing the number of slower services or imposing speed restrictions – had been taken to protect fast trains in adverse weather conditions. However, the main problem had been that the coal train and the express passed several signals that had not returned to 'danger', their arms having got stuck in the 'off' ('clear') position. The inspecting officer suggested that signals should instead be maintained at 'danger', being cleared only when a train was due. It was the beginning of the all-important 'fail-safe' principle, whereby any critical equipment must be designed such that a failure will result in a safe condition. With this in mind, the use of a white light for 'clear' was later changed to the more familiar green, lest a broken red lens fooled a driver into thinking he had an unhindered run.

If Abbots Ripton had been partly about snow, the Tay Bridge disaster would be partly about wind and rain. Designed by Thomas Bouch and built by De Bergh & Company, the elegant curving structure over the 'silvery Tay' had been lauded in the press, earned Bouch a knighthood, and had shortened the distance by rail from Edinburgh to Dundee and Aberdeen considerably. Yet the Board of Trade had expressed concern about the effect high winds might have on trains. Though some later claimed its recommended 25-mph speed restriction was inadequate, it would have been hard to predict the precise run of events that culminated in the bridge's collapse on 28 December 1879.

When the 'Mail' got to St Fort at seven that evening, the storm that had been raging all day

In the late 1870s Edward Tyer developed a 'tablet' system for protecting single-track railways. It involved installing an instrument like this one at either end of a single-track section. For a train to pass through, the signalman had to press the button to release a metal token, which was given to the driver like a passport. As the machines were interlocked with each other and with the signals, only one token could be issued at a time, and therefore only one train could be on the line at a time.

still had all the ferocity of a Turner painting. Sparks had flown forty-five minutes before, when the wheel flanges of a 'local' had been blown against the guard rail provided to prevent derailment. When the 'Mail' crossed the river, they flew again, but as the tail lamp faded away, a flash of light followed an angry gust before both train and bridge were lost to the sea.

The Court of Inquiry – the first ever convened for a railway accident – blamed the collapse of the central 'high-girder' section on the bridge's design, construction and maintenance. The Court did not ascertain precisely how it occurred, but among a number of theories is the suggestion that lateral oscillations, caused by trains passing over a track misalignment, led to fatigue cracks that reached breaking point as the 'Mail' made its final journey. Either way, the result was ruin for Bouch, and improvements to the way bridges were designed, built and inspected.

Though Tay Bridge closed a dark decade for the railways, the 1870s seeing an average of forty passengers killed each year, progress was made in other areas. The 1871 Regulation of Railways Act, for example, had finally granted the RI official powers to investigate accidents and make recommendations to prevent their recurrence. By 1873, it had been updated to require all companies to

When the central 'high-girder' section of the Tay Bridge collapsed on 28 December 1879, it took the 'Sunday Mail' with it and claimed seventy-five lives. However, the locomotive – a 4-4-0 designed by Thomas Wheatley – was salvaged, repaired and continued to haul trains until scrapped in 1919.

submit annual reports on their efforts to introduce block working and interlocked points and signals. By 1878 another Act would require companies to reveal how many of their passenger vehicles had been fitted with automatic continuous brakes.

The RI had been frustrated that the take-up of 'lock, block and brake' had been slow, yet the sheer size of the network – by now some 16,000 route miles – made any system-wide measure both time-consuming and costly. There was also some disagreement as to which braking system was most suitable, although all argument would be silenced by a terrible accident at Armagh on 12 June 1889.

Several elements made disaster likely: an overcrowded Sunday school special with no automatic brakes, hauled by an inadequately powered locomotive on a line still worked on the 'time interval' principle. Yet it would take a steep gradient and human error to make it inevitable.

In order to reach its seaside destination of Warren Point, some 24 miles away, the train first had to climb out of Armagh up an incline of 1 in 82, which steepened to 1 in 75. Services were dispatched from the terminus every ten minutes. Though the rails were dry and the engine was steaming well, the heavy load proved too much and it stalled within sight of the summit at Dobbins Bridge. The crew decided to split the train, taking the first five coaches to the top before returning for the rear ten. Unfortunately, the train was fitted with a mere 'simple' continuous brake, which meant that, when the vacuum pipe connecting the coaches was disconnected, the rear portion was held on the gradient only by the handbrake in the guard's van. Some of the wheels had been scotched with stones, but when the driver eased the engine back to aid uncoupling, it nudged the rear portion, which crunched over them and began to run back down the hill.

By this time, the next train had been dispatched from Armagh, there being no way for the signalman to know

Following spread: The terrible aftermath of the Armagh train accident of 12 June 1889. For the writer LTC Rolt, it spelled the end of 'the old happy-go-lucky days of railway working' and the start of 'the modern phase'.

that the line was blocked. Although its driver acted quickly, applying his brake as soon as he saw the runaway heading towards him, the collision could not be avoided. Eighty people were killed and 260 were injured, many of them children.

As a result, the government passed a new Regulation of Railways Act before the year was out, mandating the adoption of block signalling, the interlocking of points

and signals, and the use of automatic continuous brakes on passenger trains. Compliance would come within just a few years and would see the railways gain recognition as a relatively safe way to travel. Indeed, between 1890 and 1914 passenger and freight traffic almost doubled, but passenger fatalities fell from 249 (1880–9) to 169 (1900–9), with zero recorded for both 1901 and 1908.

Not that the trend would last.

THE DAILY MIRROR, Monday, May 24, 1915.

200 KILLED AND 300 INJURED IN RAILWAY WREC

The Daily Mirror

CERTIFIED CIRCULATION LARGER THAN ANY OTHER PICTURE PAPER IN THE WORLD

No. 3,613. | Registered at the G.P.O. as a Newspaper. | MONDAY, MAY 24, 1915 | 16 PAGES | One Halfpenny

THREE TRAINS WRECKED IN THE TERRIBLE ACCIDENT NEA CARLISLE: HEAVY DEATH ROLL AMONG THE SOLDIERS.

One of the express engines on top of the wreckage of the troop train. The tender, which is being raised by crane, was thrown down a bank.

Burning coach. Inside the compartments are masses of flames.

The Carlisle firemen worked heroically to overcome the flames.

What is probably the worst disaster in the history of British railways occurred on Saturday between Carlisle and Gretna Green, of romantic memory. Three trains were involved. First of all a troop train from Larbert, near Falkirk, collided with a local, but horror was piled upon horror's head when an express from London cras into the debris, piling engines and carriages in indescribable confusion. Fire br out and claimed many victims, chiefly among the soldiers.

HUMAN ERRORS

E AST OF SLOUGH lay four gently curved, level lines – part of the GWR's high-speed route from London to the west. In 1900, the area was block-worked by telegraph. The method was RI-approved, safe, and had – along with interlocking and the use of more effective brakes – helped fatality figures fall considerably across the country.

Yet what was cause for celebration could never be cause for complacency, for mistakes could – and did – still occur, often with lethal results. Around this time, most involved over-speeding, signalmen forgetting trains standing by their box, and SPADs. On 16 June 1900, a SPAD occurred on that safe section of line at Slough, when the 1:05 p.m. from Paddington was struck from behind by a Falmouth express at around 30 mph.

The signalman at Slough East had been offered the 'Falmouth' by his colleague at Dolphin, just over a mile away. He accepted the train, but sent a bell code informing the latter that the station was still occupied by the 1:05. Dolphin's signals therefore remained at 'danger', but the 'Falmouth' powered past them at over 50 mph. Seeing this, the signalman at Slough East grabbed a red flag and waved it from his window to try to catch the driver's eye. He also shouted to the station staff to get as many people out of the 1:05 as possible. That they did so – and quickly – undoubtedly saved all but five lives.

Perhaps the most disturbing thing about Slough was not that the driver didn't obey the signals, but that he couldn't

Opposite: How the *Daily Mirror* reported Britain's worst ever railway accident, at Quintinshill on 22 May 1915.

On 11 November 1890 the signalman at Norton Fitzwarren forgot a waiting goods train and allowed an express on to the same section of line. Ten were killed in the subsequent collision. The RI said that such accidents could be minimised by the adoption of a metal collar that could be slipped over a signal lever to stop the signalman pulling it off absentmindedly. However, many companies refused to accept this cheap, simple solution, fearing that signalmen might become over-reliant on it and drop their guard.

The devastation at Slough after the SPAD and collision of 16 June 1900.

explain why. As the driver's eyesight was found to be in good order, the inspecting officer, Lieutenant-Colonel Yorke, suggested that fatigue and age (the driver was fifty-nine) may have contributed to the error. As a result, he recommended that all drivers – 'or at any rate those employed on express trains' – undergo a medical examination at fifty-five 'and each succeeding year thereafter'.

Odd, though, that he should seem blind to the advantages of mechanical train-protection systems, despite acknowledging that *three* people on the train – the driver, fireman and guard – had not been as vigilant in their watch for signals as they should have been. Yet his fears that drivers might become over-reliant on any such device (compounded by concerns over the reliability of the equipment) were not shared by the GWR, which began to develop apparatus that would sound a bell in the cab if a Distant signal was 'clear' and a siren if it was at 'caution'. This recognised that – as trains were getting faster – Distant signals were becoming more important, as they gave drivers more time to start slowing for a Stop signal up ahead.

The in-cab side of the GWR's ATC equipment, showing the bell and siren arrangement, the bell signifying a 'clear' Distant signal, the siren indicating 'caution'.

On 12 September 1906, a mail train passed a series of signals at danger and derailed at Grantham. Fourteen people were killed. It is likely that station staff failed to connect the vacuum brake pipe correctly when the engine was changed at Peterborough, leaving the engine brake as the only one in operation. The crew were probably unaware of the problem until they tried to stop at Grantham.

Trialled on the Henley branch in 1906, the equipment was later developed so that, if a driver passed a 'caution' and failed to acknowledge the warning, the brakes would automatically apply. In this form, what became known as Automatic Train Control (ATC) would be fitted to 3,250 locomotives and 2,850 Great Western track miles by 1939 and would contribute a great deal to the company's excellent safety record. Indeed, it would be the forerunner of every train-protection system that came after; some would also come to be used to help the over-speeding problem, as we shall see. The problem of signalmen forgetting trains standing near their box would be solved more quickly, though – as with ATC – it would be an accident that took technology forward.

Traffic was heavy that Christmas Eve morning in 1910, as the rain beat down on the signal box at Hawes Junction. As well as expresses and goods trains, the signalman had a number of light engines to deal with, this being the point where the Midland Railway provided dedicated locomotives to assist trains up the punishing grade to Ais Gill. At twenty-past five, a coupled pair of these 'bankers' was allowed on to the Down (northbound) main line to

Scott Series Nº 86   THE TERRIBLE RAILWAY ACCIDENT AT GRANTHAM
THE WRECK OF THE MAIL VAN

wait for the road. Twenty-three minutes and two goods trains passed before the driver of the leading one saw the signals clear. He opened the regulator and began his journey back to Carlisle. The trouble was, the signalman had actually cleared the signals for the 'Scotch Express', which was coming up behind on the same line.

The engines had just passed through Moorcock Tunnel when the driver of the rear one looked back and saw two headlamps flickering in the darkness. But by then it was too late: the collision destroyed the first two carriages of the express, while a small fire soon worsened when escaping gas fed the flames. Twelve people were killed, some of whom had survived the crash but burned to death in the wreckage.

The RI concluded that the accident had been caused in the first instance by the signalman forgetting that he had allowed the two light engines on to the main line, and in the second by the crews of those engines forgetting to perform 'Rule 55'. This mandated the driver of a train waiting at a signal to send his fireman, guard or any other crew member to the signal box to remind the signalman of the train's presence and to make sure he put a collar on the relevant signal lever to prevent it being pulled to allow another train on to the same section of line.

The solution to this forgetfulness came in the form of track circuiting, which works by insulating sections of track at the rail joints and passing a low-voltage current through each one; this operates a relay or switch, which is held in the closed position by the current. When a train enters a section, it short-circuits the rails, opens the switch and illuminates a bulb in the signal box to indicate its presence. If a failure occurs or the circuit breaks for some other reason, the switch is also opened, meaning that – again – the system 'fails safe'.

Though patented by American engineer William Robinson in 1872, track circuiting had made little progress, largely as it was so expensive to install. After Hawes Junction, however, the Midland Railway identified two thousand locations where track circuits should be provided and duly set about installing them. The Midland was also beginning to introduce a 'rotary interlocking block system', which held a signalman's furthermost ('section') signal at 'danger', until he received positive confirmation that the previous train had reached the next box section along. It was a proactive move designed to plug gaps in the company's defences, though neither initiative would have prevented a second accident on the same line three years later.

The difference between Hawes Junction and the collision at nearby Ais Gill on 2 September 1913 was that the latter was caused by a series of SPADs. Like the former, the Midland's policy of using small engines was part of the chain, creating the need for a confusing number of light-engine moves at Hawes Junction, and leading a St Pancras-bound express to block the line by stalling at Ais Gill. And like the former, the use of gas lighting increased the death toll – this time to sixteen. Indeed, fires were becoming more frequent in post-accident situations, and Colonel Pringle – leading for the RI – urged companies to switch to electricity. Some had already started to do so, yet while around twelve thousand electrically lit vehicles were in use across Britain at this point, almost four times that number still used gas.

A Midland express passes the wreckage of the Ais Gill accident of 2 September 1913, in which a passenger train struck another that had stalled at the summit. The driver, whose train passed several signals at danger before the collision, was sentenced to two months in prison. He was granted a royal pardon after serving just nine days, many believing the company to have escaped its share of responsibility for the accident.

Pringle also advocated the construction of coaching stock with steel underframes and shock-absorbing buffers, and recommended the use of detonator placers to warn drivers who had passed red signals. But though ATC would have prevented the SPADs that led to Ais Gill, he seemed to share Yorke's view, noting that the system had not 'been proved to be efficient' and could therefore not be recommended 'as a panacea for all difficulties'; in that, at least, Pringle was right: ATC could not have prevented what became the worst accident Britain had ever known.

The first block instruments had two positions – 'Line Clear' and 'Train on Line'. These were later joined by a third – 'Line Blocked' – which became the default (or 'normal') position, and was similar in effect to keeping the signals at danger until a train was due.

Ostensibly, it's a story about two signalmen: George Meakin and James Tinsley. In reality, it's also about the First World War, which Britain had been fighting since 4 August 1914. By 22 May the following year, the conflict was putting great strain on the railways, bringing more traffic and more stress to beleaguered staff. That morning, two Glasgow-bound services were running late, so Meakin decided to shunt the local Carlisle–Beattock train out of the way at Quintinshill, a Caledonian Railway block post with no station or track circuits. Tinsley – who lived in the railway cottages at Gretna – had taken a free ride on it and arrived at around 6:30 a.m. If they'd been working according to regulations, he would have taken over from Meakin at six, but – like many others across the country – they had agreed that the one working 'earlies' could arrive a bit later, if the other covered for him by writing all subsequent train movements on a piece of paper. The 'day man' would copy the entries into the train register when he got

in, making it look like the changeover had come at the right time.

As the Down loop was holding a goods train, Meakin decided to put the 'local' on the Up Main. Though not an ideal move, it wasn't dangerous if the proper precautions were taken – that is, if he sent a bell code to Kirkpatrick signal box to let its signalman know that the running line was occupied, and placed a collar over the signal lever to stop himself allowing another train on to the same section of line. Today, he forgot – but even then all would have been well had the fireman of the 'local' performed 'Rule 55' properly; but the fireman merely signed the register while Tinsley was trying to copy Meakin's scribbled train movements into it. The fact that two brakesmen were also in the box, chatting with Meakin about the war, probably didn't help Tinsley's concentration either.

Between the passage of the first Glasgow express and his own acceptance of the second, Tinsley accepted an Up troop train from Kirkpatrick. It was just before ten-to seven when it struck the 'local' waiting on the same line, and just after when the second express ploughed into the wreckage. In all, 227 people were killed and 246 were injured.

That Meakin and Tinsley were imprisoned for negligence overlooks the multi-causal nature of the accident. It was clear, for one thing, that the signalmen were poorly supervised; clear too that the war had not only created a need for more and more military traffic, but also forced the Caledonian to press old Great Central Railway stock into service, whose wooden bodies, wooden frames and gas lighting ensured that – as with Hawes Junction and Ais Gill – fire increased the death toll.

The war would have another, longer-lasting, effect on the railways, helping end the era of small private companies and start another of large corporations.

Yet the problems of SPADs, speed and signalmen's errors would remain.

Opposite:
On 26 January 1921, an accident occurred near Abermule that demonstrated the dangers of single-line working. Despite the use of Tyer's tablet system, confusion at the station led to the driver of one train being given back the token he had just handed over. As the instrument at the other end of the section was therefore not locked out, it let the signalman there issue a token for a train coming the other way. Seventeen people were killed in the inevitable head-on collision.

TAKING CONTROL

BEHIND A HUGE desk sits the Honourable Charles Napier Lawrence. Sporting a frock-coat and winged collar, he looks from the window as he ponders the future of his new company. For him, there will be elevation to the peerage; for the company, there will be grime, glory and – at least to start with – in-fighting and feuds. The date is 1 January 1923; the company is the London Midland & Scottish Railway – the LMS. Lawrence is its first chairman. He is not a man to be envied.

Like the London & North Eastern (LNER) and Southern (SR) railways, the LMS had been created under the 'Grouping' of some 120 smaller companies by a government seeking to stem financial losses and retain the

benefits of wartime unity. Its early years were characterised by financial difficulty and disagreement – generally between its two largest constituents, the LNWR and the Midland. Lawrence had chaired the former, but it was generally the will of the latter that prevailed, many Midland practices being adopted as policies by the LMS board. Sometimes this was beneficial, such as the decision to follow that company's centralised traffic management system; sometimes it was less so, as in the continuation of its small-engine strategy. The latter had been a contributory factor to the collisions at Hawes Junction and Ais Gill, but only really started to change when economic pressures started to mount: small engines were unable to cope with heavy trains and steep inclines alone, so double-heading, piloting and banking moves were required, which were expensive and had begun to affect punctuality. The solution began with the powerful 'Royal Scot' class, introduced from 1927, and continued with the famous 'Pacific' fleets built the following decade.

Reorganisation often delays industrial progress as new feet find their faltering way. And at first the Grouping had a detrimental effect on braking systems: up to around 1914, Britain's railways had three vacuum-braked carriages for every two equipped with air brakes, but freedom from manufacturing rights and patent liabilities had led the

The first move away from the old Midland 'small-engine' policy came in 1927 with the launch of the 'Royal Scot' class, the first of which – no. 6100 – is seen resplendent in this period postcard.

L.M.S.
"ROYAL SCOT"

'Big Four' to standardise on the former. It was a mistake, as vacuum brakes take longer to react than air brakes, particularly over a long train, and therefore need a direct admission valve on each vehicle, which makes them more expensive to install and maintain.

The Grouping also put the brakes on the quest for automatic train control. By now, the Great Western (the only one of the 'Big Four' to have survived virtually intact) was not alone in seeking to cut the number of SPADs. The North Eastern, for example, had fitted mechanical devices at Distant signals on ninety of its route miles and equipped over 1,500 locomotives to activate them. The Great Central, Great Eastern, LB&SCR and LNWR were also conducting experiments, but – almost overnight – everything stopped. Why? It certainly wasn't down to a drop in SPADs, which resulted in five fatalities in 1923 alone, nor to a lack of official backing. It wasn't down to a lack of consideration either, a committee – chaired by Colonel Pringle – having been set up in 1920 to look into the whole subject.

Ironically, the trouble came when the committee published its conclusions two years later. While they saw the benefits that warning devices at Distant signals could bring, they felt 'trip-stop' controls at certain Stop signals to be more important. They also suggested that companies

During William Stanier's tenure as LMS Chief Mechanical Engineer, the company not only continued the 'larger engine' concept but also increased train speeds. Faster trains, though, require more efficient brakes: when the LMS broke the speed record in June 1937 by reaching 114 mph with a special hauled by no. 6220 *Coronation*, disaster nearly struck when the driver failed to apply them and took the train through Crewe's 25-mph crossovers at 57.

On 22 March 1931, six people died and twenty-six were injured when a Euston–Glasgow express derailed while crossing from the Down Fast to the Down Slow line at Leighton Buzzard. Its driver had passed a signal at danger and failed to apply the brakes. ATC would probably have stopped the train before it reached the points.

should co-operate and provide standard equipment to indicate whether a signal was at 'danger', 'caution' or 'clear'. In short, they over-complicated the issue by being over-ambitious – and ambition cost money the Big Four didn't have, the end of the war having brought huge rises in labour and materials costs, and greater competition from road hauliers. Savings could have been made if the committee had concentrated on Distant signals and if the other companies had simply adopted the Great Western's ATC, but it hadn't, they didn't, and SPADs continued to cause accidents. One came on 13 October 1928, just twelve days after Pringle had chaired the first meeting of a second ATC committee. It doubtless focused the minds of its members – particularly the two from the LMS, on whose territory it took place …

The mist was still rising over Charfield as a goods train was setting back into a siding. Though visibility was poor,

the signalman knew it wasn't bad enough to summon a fog man to keep watch. Had he done so, and had that man put a detonator down when the Distant was at 'caution', the driver of the 10:00 p.m. Leeds–Bristol might not have passed the Stop signal at 'danger'. As it was, the 'Bristol' entered the section at speed, grazed two of the wagons, collided with the engine and careered into the path of a passing empty freight. Almost immediately, escaping gas began to burn, the flames being fuelled by the wooden bodies of the carriages and wagons. Fifteen people died.

Pringle's investigation revealed that half the LMS's passenger vehicles were still gas-lit. He pressed for conversion to electricity, but also acknowledged that ATC 'alone [could] prevent the occurrence of accidents due to misreading of signals, or to failures of enginemen to observe and obey signals'. His second committee's report – published in 1930 – supported the view, and proposed various 'indirect' ways of helping crews, like the use of electrically powered colour-light signals, which were not only easier to see in fog, but also required less maintenance. The LMS and Southern favoured this option; the Great Western did not, and carried on equipping its main lines with ATC, pleased that its own system had been endorsed. The LNER introduced an electrical relay interlocking system between Northallerton and York, but though the installation of track circuits and block signalling continued, looming economic depression and expanding road haulage empires meant that money for investment in new safety systems remained scarce. Even so, the decade began well, with only one fatal train accident (Culgaith, 6 March 1930) and an average of around eight passenger fatalities each year for the next four years. Then, on Saturday 15 June 1935, came a collision that showed it wasn't only driver errors that caused problems.

The evening was dark and drizzly as a Newcastle express approached Welwyn at speed. Seeing the Distant at

The wreckage of the accident at Welwyn Garden City, as recorded by the *Daily Mirror*.

Opposite: The accident at Dolphin Junction, Slough, in 1941 was caused by the signalman failing to ensure that an approaching freight train had stopped at the protecting signal before authorising a passenger train to cross its path. Five were killed and twenty-four were injured in the collision.

'caution', its driver shut off steam and applied the brakes. As the train rumbled along at 20 mph, he saw the arm of the home signal rise, so he opened up again and the train began to accelerate. But the signals weren't for him, they were for a Leeds-bound service coming up on the same line. The signalman had accepted it from the previous box in error. Fourteen people were killed and eighty-one were injured when the rear-end collision came.

The RI judged that the signalman had become confused, and recommended altering the interlocking so that a second train could not be accepted until the first had definitely passed through the section. This was achieved by linking the track circuit at the first Stop signal beyond the Distant to the block indicator so that 'Line Clear' could not be given until the circuit had been occupied and then cleared again. This so-called 'Welwyn Control' was widely adopted and closed a loophole in the 'absolute block' system. It also illustrates how safety devices and methods develop over time, for though it may take one accident to bring invention, perfection usually takes more. The same was true of train control, for though ATC seemed to ease the SPAD problem, it did not solve it, as the events of 4 November 1940 would demonstrate.

It was a black night in Norton Fitzwarren, Somerset, though the blackout made it blacker still. A sleeping-car train was heading towards Penzance on the Relief line. It usually ran on the 'Main', but was so late that the signalman at Taunton West had re-routed it to give a newspaper train, which was early – and gaining on the 'sleeper' – a clear run.

When the same thing happens day after day, week in, week out, it's easy to fall into the trap of familiarity. The 'sleeper' *always* ran on the 'Main'; the driver *always* looked at the same signal. Tonight he looked at the same signal and it was 'off'. But it wasn't for him; his own Relief line signal was 'on', and the trap points protecting the 'Main' were set for the run-off. They were just 350 yards away.

The 'newspaper' continued to catch up, until both trains were running side by side. It was now that the driver of the 'sleeper' realised his mistake. He slammed on the brakes and the metal screamed...too late: the engine tore into the earth and the first six carriages were thrown across all four lines like toys. Of the nine hundred passengers aboard, twenty-seven were killed.

It hadn't just been a case of 'right track, wrong signal'; the investigation concluded that the driver must have unconsciously cancelled the ATC warning at Norton's Distant signal too. Again, war played its part, German bombing having begun to eat away at the country for the second time in a generation. One such raid had recently destroyed the driver's house.

With 'Welwyn control', the berth track circuit at the home signal must be occupied then cleared before another 'Line Clear' can be given. This can be circumvented by 'winding the Welwyn' (shown here), if necessary, to overcome a failure.

NATIONALISATION, MODERNISATION AND THE THREAT OF FOG

ALTHOUGH AN AIR raid was partly responsible for Norton Fitzwarren, enemy action often had a more direct impact on the railway. On 10 July 1940, for example, a train was bombed near Newhaven, killing the driver and injuring the guard, while a strike on Hungerford Bridge in London four years later prevented the normal passage of trains for six months.

Peace in 1945 brought a desire for change, the new Labour government favouring the public ownership

of public services. As a result, the 1947 Transport Act heralded the nationalisation of the GWR, LMS, LNER and Southern (along with fifty smaller companies) from 1 January 1948. The system was divided into six regions, above which sat an 'executive', one of five answering to the British Transport Commission (BTC).

Trading as 'British Railways' (BR), the Railway Executive knew it had to renew worn-out locomotives and rolling stock, but the need to continue restoring the track to pre-war standards often led to diversions that took drivers down less familiar lines. That this increased the risk from accidents had been demonstrated disastrously at Bourne End on Sunday 30 September 1945.

Because of engineering works in Watford Tunnel, London-bound trains were being routed from the Fast line to the Slow. The LMS had equipped the section with semaphore Stop signals, but used a colour-light Distant, which showed two yellows if a train was to cross over. Just after nine that morning, a fifteen-car express from Perth failed to slow down and derailed on the points. The locomotive and several carriages plunged down a nine-foot embankment. The driver, fireman and forty-one passengers lost their lives.

Investigating for the RI, Lieutenant-Colonel Sir Alan Mount noted that sunlight on the driver's face might have made the 'double yellow' more difficult to see. He also saw ambiguity in the LMS Rule Book, which said only that two yellows '*may* denote that points are set for a diverging route' (author's italics). The LMS reacted by removing the ambiguity and would soon abandon the 'double-yellow' indication ahead of junctions. For Mount, though, Bourne End brought up the question of Automatic Train Control once more.

There was a danger, said some, that ATC would divert resources from the modernisation of signals and installation of track circuits. Within three years, however, the

Opposite: Seeing a fire in the leading wagon of his ammunition train at Soham on 2 June 1944, Driver Benjamin Gimbert stopped and told his fireman, James Nightall, to uncouple it. Gimbert had hauled the isolated wagon some 140 yards when the bombs on board went off. The explosion killed Nightall; Gimbert was badly injured. Although the station was nearly destroyed and seven hundred properties were damaged, the men had saved the town from a much worse fate and were awarded George Medals.

The Bourne
End disaster of
30 September
1945.

An official GWR
photograph
showing the
derailment at
Wootton Bassett
Junction on
27 June 1946.

positive-thinking, all-new Railway Executive had announced its intention to fit what it called (more accurately) 'Warning Control' to all main-line routes. Alas, when it became clear that there was no money for such a wide-reaching programme, it was forced to back-pedal, promising to address the issue 'as soon as circumstances … allowed'.

BR had inherited almost 3,000 miles of ex-GWR track fitted with its mechanically based ATC system, and 37 miles between London and Southend, on which the LMS had installed a similar set-up, activated by magnetic induction. Seeking to make progress, the Executive entered into several studies, experiments and trials to find the final form that 'Warning Control' should take. ATC was favoured at first, but its need for mechanical contact was thought to be a disadvantage at high speed; there was also a possibility of false indications being given by stray earth currents in electrified areas. It was therefore decided to adapt the LMS system, although it proved very difficult to make the desired modifications and the design was not finalised until August 1952. Before the first test run could be made, an accident occurred on 8 October that would raise the profile of the whole project.

Though the fatality count at Harrow & Wealdstone was high, the collision demonstrated the strength of BR's new 'Mark I' carriages, two of which – featuring the latest arrangement of all-steel welded body mounted on a 200-ton end-load resistant underframe – were in the train from Euston.

Like Harrow & Wealdstone, the accident at Lewisham on 4 December 1957 also arose from a SPAD, which also led to a rear-end collision. In this case, however, the consequences were compounded by a bridge strike and collapse.

There can be no doubt that fog played a part. London had always been known for it, but when combined with smoke from factories and the burning fires of home, it became smog and could be lethal. At Harrow & Wealdstone station that morning, visibility had improved a little as the sun began to rise, but was still only 50–100 yards at the Distant signal.

Shortly after 8:15 a.m., a commuter train from Tring pulled in and waited. Its nine coaches were packed with eight hundred passengers; many more were getting ready to board. Some would have only ninety seconds left to live. At 8:19, an express from Perth burst out of the murk, over the points and struck it with such force that the last three coaches were crushed to the length of little more than one, and the whole train was pushed forward around 20 yards.

Although the signalman acted quickly in returning his signals to 'danger', a Euston–Liverpool/Manchester service ran into the wreckage soon after. In all, there were 112 fatalities – a death toll second only to Quintinshill.

The investigation report confirmed that the Perth train had passed the colour-light Distant at 'caution' and two semaphore signals at 'danger'. Its author, Lieutenant-Colonel Wilson, urged BR to continue with its 'Warning Control' programme, which clearly could have prevented the accident. Prior to publication, the BTC had announced that – as soon as the equipment was working satisfactorily – it would launch a five-year plan to fit 1,332 miles of main line, with a further 4,000 miles earmarked for the longer term. 'Warning Control' (or AWS, the Automatic Warning System) was fitted between King's Cross and Grantham in 1956, by which time the scheme had been embodied in the BTC's 'Modernisation Plan', which set aside £1,200 million to be spent on greater mechanisation, more colour-light signalling, permanent way improvements, and the substitution of steam by diesel and electric traction.

By 1960, AWS had reached York, and would soon spread to other routes. In time, it would help reduce the number of fatalities in train accidents, although some of the new technologies that came in the wake of modernisation would bring problems of their own.

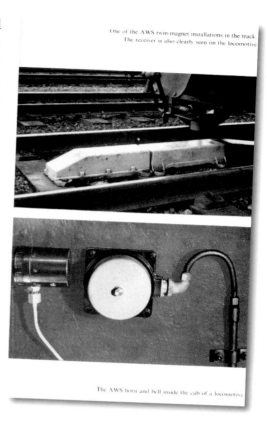

One of the AWS twin-magnet installations in the track. The receiver is also clearly seen on the locomotive

The AWS horn and bell inside the cab of a locomotive

Taken from an official BR booklet, the upper image shows a twin AWS magnet in the track and the receiver attached to a locomotive. The lower image shows the AWS bell and horn, as fitted inside a locomotive cab.

NEW RAILWAY, NEW DANGER?

A DARK BREEZY night in February 1961, and a freight train is powering from Woodford to Mottram at just over 50 mph. Unbeknown to the driver, one wagon – a steel-framed pallet van – begins to sway, its movement increasing until the wheels leave the rails just north of Rugby. More wagons come off as the train clatters on, but after a mile or so the coupling breaks and the trucks are left foul of the adjacent line. As the front portion heads for Lutterworth, it passes a passenger service coming the other way. No one could have known that it would soon strike the wagons, that its engine would overturn and that its driver would be killed.

Derailments involving short-wheelbase wagons running at speed on plain line would be something of a theme in the 1960s. These vehicles had been running across Britain without incident for many years, so what had changed? The answer lay partly in the wagon, partly in the track and partly in the traction type – all of which could be summed up in one word: modernisation.

BR's Modernisation Plan had seen the introduction of more steel-framed wagons and continuous welded rail (CWR). The former were easier to maintain, the latter gave a smoother, quieter ride, but together they exacerbated the phenomenon of 'hunting' – a lateral wheel oscillation at the root of many derailments. The trouble was that steel-framed wagons were less flexible than their older counterparts, making them more prone to a build-up of oscillations following any imperfections in the track.

Opposite: The aftermath of the fatal collision at Hixon on 6 January 1968. The accident stalled British Rail's level-crossing automation programme until the late 1970s, when the Court of Inquiry recommendations were reassessed.

The aftermath of the derailment and collision at Rugby on 11 February 1961.

On 31 July 1967, a short-wheelbase wagon in a freight train began to 'hunt', leading it and other wagons to derail foul of the adjacent line at Thirsk. Though the driver of an approaching express applied his brakes, it collided with the wagons, killing seven people and injuring forty-five more.

Being laid on concrete sleepers, CWR introduced even more rigidity, while its lack of joints meant fewer natural breaks to disrupt the effect. When these factors combined with the sustained high speeds possible with diesel traction and continuous braking, incidents increased alarmingly.

Yet these consequences were unintended, could not have been foreseen and needed a new way of thinking to deal with them. And that's what happened, specialist research leading to a new suspension system that could combat

'hunting' and achieve good ride quality on all types of track. However, there was one problem brought about by modernisation that might perhaps have been anticipated.

Level crossings date back to the earliest horse-drawn tramway systems. Some of Tyneside's eighteenth-century wooden wagonways also had gated crossing points from which a 'keeper' would oversee manoeuvres. Originally, the gates were kept closed across the line, but in 1834 the Liverpool & Manchester Railway started to block the road during the daytime. BR was legally obliged to maintain attendance at all public level crossings, which was expensive – and difficult, near full employment after the war making it hard to find staff for what was a responsible, but poorly paid and often dull job.

By 1955, there were over three million cars on British roads, and the number was rising. Many crossings took time to operate, caused heavy delays and offered insufficient protection for such an increase in usage. Clearly the situation was only going to get worse. Something had to be done, and the answer seemed to lie on the Continent.

The RI – along with representatives from BR and the Ministry of Transport – reviewed European automatic level crossings in detail the following year. The group's

At Hither Green on 5 November 1967, a piece of rail broke away as a train passed at 70 mph. When the derailed wheels struck a crossover, four coaches overturned and forty-nine passengers died. Though the cause was the way the track had been supported, it was realised more generally that the smaller wheels of diesel and electric locomotives and units, combined with the high unsprung weight resulting from their axle-hung traction motors, had a more punishing effect on the track than steam locomotives.

findings led to the creation of the attendant-free automatic half-barrier crossing – or AHB – whose closure sequence was activated by an approaching train via a treadle attached to the rail. Though there was some opposition to these 'Continental crossings', which many feared were not safe, the first AHB came into use at Spath, near Uttoxeter, on 5 February 1961. By the end of 1967, there were 207, with plans for many more. Then came an accident that highlighted the shortcomings of both the design itself, and the way it had been introduced.

Its police escort already across, on 6 January 1968 a colossal road transporter carrying a 120-ton transformer was crawling carefully over Hixon AHB. At around 12:30 p.m., the red lights started to flash and the barriers began to lower. The driver had failed to phone the signalman; the vehicle failed to get clear. It was struck by an express at around 75 mph. Eleven people were killed, 120 yards of track were damaged, and the overhead power lines were brought down.

Hixon was only the second accident – Tay Bridge being the first – to be subject to a Court of Inquiry. Here, the Attorney General, Sir Elwyn Jones, is seen during a recess on 26 February 1968.

Realising that the RI's involvement in the AHB's development compromised its independence, the government chose to hold a Court of Inquiry under the Regulation of Railways Act 1871, appointing Mr E. B. Gibbens QC as chair. The first since Tay Bridge, the Court found that the haulage company had failed to inform BR that it intended to take the transporter over the crossing, which in turn prevented BR from taking appropriate precautions. However, while highlighting poor communications between both railway and police and railway and haulier about the need to telephone the signalman in such cases, and while citing inadequate signs and poor police training as part of the causal chain, it found the 'origin of the accident' to be 'the failure of officers of both the Ministry and British Railways in collaboration to appreciate the measures necessary to deal with a hazard of which they were aware'.

Because of the many management failings beneath Hixon's surface, the inquiry recommended several additional safety measures, whose cost stalled the automation policy severely: indeed, although better signage and warning lights were introduced from 1969, little progress would be made until 1977, when another working party visited Europe and agreed to relax the recommendation requirements. It also endorsed an automatic crossing that had warning lights, but no barriers. Forty-four of these automatic 'open' crossings were in use by 1986. Though cheap to install and maintain, they did let road users cross the railway when it only *seemed* safe to do so. The dangers were demonstrated at Lockington that same year, when eight rail passengers and a boy travelling in a van were killed when the van driver missed the lights and drove into the path of a train.

Such was the shape of things to come, but in 1969 BR was focusing on competing with the rise of private car ownership and increasingly affordable domestic flights, its engineers having applied the suspension derived from the 'hunting' research to a new coach capable of 125-mph travel. At the same time, AWS had spread to some 3,000 track miles, while more track circuiting and regularly spaced colour-light signals were reducing the risk from SPADs. The trouble was, drivers didn't only need reminding about red signals.

At 9:15 a.m. on 9 September 1968, the crew of a light locomotive were killed when it struck the rear of a passenger train at Castlecary in Scotland. The RI determined that the signalman, when telling the driver to pass a signal at 'danger', had become confused as to which driver he was speaking, and had failed to tell him to proceed at caution.

RETURN TO CLAPHAM

Morpeth, county town of Northumberland, is also the site of a curve with a radius of just 285 metres. Sharp curves mean lower speeds – in this case 40 mph. Most of the time, the restriction is observed, the brakes are applied and the train remains upright. On 7 May 1969, however, a driver had been handed an official letter requesting reasons for time lost on a previous journey. It played on his mind; he was a good, conscientious man.

Still, when he took over the Down 'Aberdonian' at Newcastle, he could be confident that he knew the road, knew his locomotive and knew his job. Progress was good, and as the train passed Stannington, he shut off power, allowing the 'Deltic' to coast towards the curve; it was then that he started to think about that letter again, then that he forgot to apply the brake…The train rounded the bend at 80 and the sparks began to fly. Five passengers and a ticket inspector were killed when it derailed.

The RI recommended that AWS be fitted to warn drivers of severe speed restrictions on high-speed lines. BR adopted the proposal in the wider sense, but did not provide the equipment on the Up line at Morpeth as it failed to meet the fitment criteria, featuring a 'cascade' of descending speed restrictions, rather than a single one, as on the 'Down'. A second – non-fatal – derailment on the 'Up' in June 1984 caused this to be changed, although a further non-fatal speed-related accident there in 1994 suggested that AWS was not necessarily the answer. Back in

Opposite:
This photograph of the derailment at Morpeth in 1969 also shows the nature of the curve, whose radius reduces to just 285 metres at its sharpest point.

the 1970s, though, it was one of the best weapons in BR's arsenal, and an accident at Nuneaton on 6 June 1975 would see it given yet another use.

On 22 February 1971, a passenger train failed to stop at Sheerness and overrode the buffer stops in the bay platform. Thirteen people were injured, and a woman standing in the booking hall was killed. The RI determined the most likely cause to be that the driver had lost consciousness moments before the collision.

Following track remodelling, the speed limit just south of the station was temporarily lowered to 20 mph. About a mile ahead of the affected area sat a warning board to remind drivers to start slowing down. It should have been lit, but the gas had run out. This fooled the driver of a sleeping-car train into thinking that normal line speed had been restored. He kept his speed steady at around 80; by the time the board marking the start of the actual restriction came into view, it was too late. The driver braked hard, but the train derailed and its coaches were scattered in all directions. Six people were killed and thirty-eight were injured.

AWS seemed a simple, ideal solution, but there was a danger that using it ahead of sharp curves, speed restrictions *and* signals could lead to over-familiarity, and a situation where a driver might reset the equipment

almost subconsciously after receiving a warning. Doing so without thinking at a 'yellow' might lead to the same thing happening at a 'red', which could lead to a SPAD – and a collision. Fear of this kept Southern Region managers away from AWS for many years, as they knew that one 'yellow' was very likely to lead to another on their busy suburban network – especially at peak periods.

Though AWS undoubtedly had its limitations, its reach (3,200 track miles in 1970; 7,013 in 1989) was undoubtedly helping to cut the number of accidents, as were improvements in route learning and a greater understanding of what is now called the 'wheel-rail interface'. But while not a single passenger fatality occurred in 1976 or 1977, the railway could not afford to be complacent. Indeed, a sleeper-train fire that claimed twelve lives at Taunton in 1978 resulted from poor staff training and supervision,

On 19 December 1973, an incorrectly secured battery-box door on a locomotive opened and struck point machinery at Longfield Avenue Junction, near West Ealing. The resulting derailment led to the loss of ten lives.

On 28 February 1975, an Underground train failed to slow on the approach to Moorgate station. It overran the platform, before colliding with the buffer stops and striking the end wall beyond. Forty-three people were killed, including the driver. Medical evidence said it was possible he had been affected by amnesia. The accident led to the introduction of 'Moorgate Control', which comprises a series of trainstops, linked to timers, designed to stop trains travelling over a certain speed on the approach to buffer stops. This shot shows the entrance to Platform 9, where rescue workers are using cutting equipment try to free passengers from the wreckage.

the use of non-fire-retardant materials in the coach where the fire started, and – most worryingly – a failure to share lessons learnt after a similar incident on a different region of BR.

Aside from various measures, such as the introduction of tighter maintenance procedures, many of the issues raised by Taunton would be addressed by new 'Mark III' sleeping cars, with their improved materials, signage, refined fire-alarm systems and smoke detectors.

The basic 'Mark III' coach was winning passengers at this time as part of BR's 'Inter-City 125' High Speed Trains (HST). By 1979, they were also being used on accelerated services between Glasgow and Edinburgh, but as there were insufficient funds for full HST sets, BR adopted a 'push-pull' formation, with a Class 47 diesel-electric at one end of the train and a lightweight driving trailer (effectively a 'Mark II' coach with a cab) at the other. Passengers were delighted with the 100-mph top speed and the comparative luxury of the 'Mark IIIs' – until, that is, the early evening of 30 July 1984, when a Glasgow express (driving trailer leading) struck a cow that had got through a hole in the boundary fence near Polmont. Thirteen people were killed.

Post-accident response training under way at Swindon Works in 1978.

Though chance played a large part in this accident – a specific part of the cow had to be struck at a specific moment, on a specific trajectory to lift the wheel with sufficient force to derail the train – BR learnt several lessons quickly. Before long, it would introduce cab-to-shore radios,

The aftermath of the collision between a push-pull passenger train and a cow near Polmont on 30 July 1984. Thirteen people were killed. Note, however, how the 'Mark III' carriages have retained their structural integrity; this is due to their computer-based design, which served to optimise strength and stiffness – a very 'crashworthy' combination.

improve the fencing along its main lines, and add extra weight to its driving trailers (a policy carried on to later designs, high-speed push-pull operation also being planned for the East and West Coast main lines at the time).

BR's reaction to Polmont might be said to reflect a period of greater optimism in the industry. Indeed, the 'sectorisation' that had seen it create five separate business units would soon start to pay off, and what with work on the Channel Tunnel having begun, the electrification of the East Coast main line under way, rising passenger numbers and falling subsidies, it seemed that a golden age could be dawning. Then came Clapham.

By the late 1980s, resignalling schemes had been commissioned or completed at Brighton, Newcastle, York, Leeds, Leicester and Waterloo. The last was a particularly big operation, involving the replacement of equipment on the busiest stretch of railway in Britain. On the evening of 27 November 1988, an overtired, under-trained technician left a bare live wire dangling in a relay room at Clapham Junction 'A', a huge signal box on a gantry that spanned a sea of lines at the station throat. Two weeks later, further work jolted the wire, causing it to touch a terminal, make a connection and prevent a signal from returning to 'danger' after the passage of a train.

Just after 8 a.m. on Monday 12 December, a commuter service was heading for the cutting where that signal stood. Green light followed green light: the usual story – except that the last one should have been red…As the train rounded the curve into the cutting, its driver saw another blocking the line ahead. He applied the emergency brake, but it was too late. The collision forced the leading coach to the side, where it struck an empty unit passing on the opposite line. Thirty-five people were killed and almost five hundred were injured.

The chairman of BR, Sir Robert Reid, visited the crash site and accepted full responsibility on behalf of the company. He knew there was much to be done, but within a few months the questions some had raised on the eve of sectorisation about standards, staff cuts and chains of command would come up again when two fatal SPADs occurred in just three days (Purley, 4 March 1989; and Bellgrove, 6 March 1989). The Clapham inquiry – chaired by Sir Anthony Hidden QC – also looked at common issues arising from these SPADs, and led to changes in signal-testing procedures and working hours for 'safety critical' staff.

Though Clapham Junction was a catalyst for Automatic Train Protection, it had actually been proposed in October 1988, two months before the accident. This view shows the post-accident clearance operation.

By 1990, the goods driver with whom we began could look forward to a new era, in which BR would improve its whole safety culture by identifying clear lines of responsibility. It would also ensure that 'risk management' and 'change management' played a vital part in the decision-making process, and that work was accelerated on an Automatic Train Protection system (ATP), which improved on AWS by stopping *any* train that passed a signal at danger.

Yet our driver might not have realised that he wouldn't be working for BR for much longer: privatisation – which split track and train by dividing the railway into around a hundred separate businesses – began in 1994. Soon after the process ended in 1997, a series of major accidents prompted questions about the way it had damaged the industry's accident defences. Of these, it would be the SPAD and collision at Ladbroke Grove on 5 October 1999 that eventually led (*inter alia*) to more robust rolling-stock designs and sped the adoption not of ATP, but the cheaper Train Protection and Warning System (TPWS), which also improves on AWS by automatically applying the brakes on a train that has passed a signal at 'danger' or is approaching one too fast.

The Hidden Report into the Clapham accident was produced by only the third Court of Inquiry in British railway history.

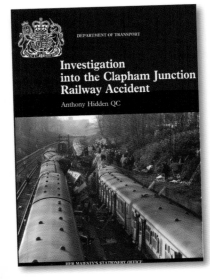

Of course, TPWS is merely one in a long line of safety improvements – from the adoption of 'lock, block and brake' by 1900, to the increasing mechanisation that has helped train accident fatalities fall since 1950. It certainly won't be the last – not in an industry where staff retire, move on, or move in from elsewhere, and where the human element still sits alongside technologies old and new. For this reason, the railway will go on monitoring trends, go on innovating, keep remembering the lessons of the past, and keep sharing those of the present – until the future means it no longer needs to.

FURTHER READING

This book is merely a summary of British railway accidents and the safety initiatives that came from them. More detailed information may be found in the following:

Coleman, Terry. *The Railway Navvies*. Penguin, 1981.

Faith, Nicholas. *Derail: Why Trains Crash*. Channel 4 Books, 2000.

Gourvish, T. R. *British Railways 1974–97: A Business History*. Cambridge University Press, 1986.

Hall, Stanley. *Railway Detectives: The 150-Year Saga of the Railway Inspectorate*. Ian Allan, 1990.

Hall, Stanley. *Beyond Hidden Dangers: Railway Safety into the 21st Century*. Ian Allan, 2003.

Hall, Stanley, and Van der Mark, Peter. *Level Crossings*. Ian Allan, 2008.

Kitchenside, G. M., and Williams, Alan. *British Railway Signalling*. Ian Allan, third edition 1980.

Lewis, Peter. *Beautiful Railway Bridge of the Silvery Tay*. The History Press, 2004.

Reason, James. *Managing the Risks of Organisational Accidents*. Ashgate Publishing, 2002.

Rolt, L. T. C. *Red for Danger*. Sutton Publishing, 1998 (first published in 1955, and updated in 1966).

Rolt, L. T. C. *George and Robert Stephenson: The Railway Revolution*. Longman, 1960.

Vaughan, Adrian. *Tracks to Disaster*. Ian Allan, 2000.

Wolmar, Christian. *Fire and Steam: A New History of the Railways in Britain*. Atlantic Books, 2007.

Most of the RI investigation reports referred to in this book may be downloaded free of charge from the Railways Archive website: www.railwaysarchive.co.uk

The RI itself became part of the Health & Safety Executive in 1990, but the Hidden Inquiry resulted in the creation of an independent Rail Accident Investigation Branch (RAIB). More information, and all RAIB's reports, may be found on its website: www.raib.gov.uk

Statistics and reports on how the modern rail industry learns from operational experience may be found on the website of RSSB – originally founded as the Rail Safety and Standards Board: www.rssb.co.uk

INDEX